IN MEMORIAM A. H. H.

By ALFRED TENNYSON

In Memoriam A. H. H.
By Alfred Tennyson

Print ISBN 13: 978-1-4209-7914-5
eBook ISBN 13: 978-1-4209-8049-3

This edition copyright © 2021. Digireads.com Publishing.

All rights reserved. No part of this publication may be reproduced, distributed, or transmitted in any form or by any means, including photocopying, recording, or other electronic or mechanical methods, without the prior written permission of the publisher, except in the case of brief quotations embodied in critical reviews and certain other noncommercial uses permitted by copyright law.

Cover Image: a detail of a portrait of Arthur Henry Hallam, English School, c. 1901 (litho) / Prismatic Pictures / Bridgeman Images.

Please visit *www.digireads.com*

IN MEMORIAM A. H. H.

OBIIT MDCCCXXXIII

Prologue

Strong Son of God, immortal Love,
   Whom we, that have not seen thy face,
   By faith, and faith alone, embrace,
Believing where we cannot prove;

Thine are these orbs of light and shade;
   Thou madest Life in man and brute;
   Thou madest Death; and lo, thy foot
Is on the skull which thou hast made.

Thou wilt not leave us in the dust:
   Thou madest man, he knows not why,
   He thinks he was not made to die;
And thou hast made him: thou art just.

Thou seemest human and divine,
   The highest, holiest manhood, thou.
   Our wills are ours, we know not how,
Our wills are ours, to make them thine.

Our little systems have their day;
   They have their day and cease to be:
   They are but broken lights of thee,
And thou, O Lord, art more than they.

We have but faith: we cannot know;
   For knowledge is of things we see;
   And yet we trust it comes from thee,
A beam in darkness: let it grow.

Let knowledge grow from more to more,
   But more of reverence in us dwell;
   That mind and soul, according well,
May make one music as before,

But vaster. We are fools and slight;
  We mock thee when we do not fear:
  But help thy foolish ones to bear;
Help thy vain worlds to bear thy light.

Forgive what seem'd my sin in me,
  What seem'd my worth since I began;
  For merit lives from man to man,
And not from man, O Lord, to thee.

Forgive my grief for one removed,
  Thy creature, whom I found so fair.
  I trust he lives in thee, and there
I find him worthier to be loved.

Forgive these wild and wandering cries,
  Confusions of a wasted youth;
  Forgive them where they fail in truth,
And in thy wisdom make me wise.

I

I held it truth, with him who sings
  To one clear harp in divers tones,
  That men may rise on stepping-stones
Of their dead selves to higher things.

But who shall so forecast the years
  And find in loss a gain to match?
  Or reach a hand thro' time to catch
The far-off interest of tears?

Let Love clasp Grief lest both be drown'd,
  Let darkness keep her raven gloss:
  Ah, sweeter to be drunk with loss,
To dance with death, to beat the ground,

Than that the victor Hours should scorn
  The long result of love, and boast,
  "Behold the man that loved and lost,
But all he was is overworn."

This truth came borne with bier and pall,
   I felt it, when I sorrow'd most,
   'Tis better to have loved and lost,
Than never to have loved at all.

II

Old Yew, which graspest at the stones
   That name the under-lying dead,
   Thy fibres net the dreamless head,
Thy roots are wrapt about the bones.

The seasons bring the flower again,
   And bring the firstling to the flock;
   And in the dusk of thee, the clock
Beats out the little lives of men.

O not for thee the glow, the bloom,
   Who changest not in any gale,
   Nor branding summer suns avail
To touch thy thousand years of gloom:

And gazing on thee, sullen tree,
   Sick for thy stubborn hardihood,
   I seem to fail from out my blood
And grow incorporate into thee.

III

O Sorrow, cruel fellowship,
   O Priestess in the vaults of Death,
   O sweet and bitter in a breath,
What whispers from thy lying lip?

"The stars," she whispers, "blindly run;
   A web is wov'n across the sky;
   From out waste places comes a cry,
And murmurs from the dying sun:

"And all the phantom, Nature, stands—
   With all the music in her tone,
   A hollow echo of my own,—
A hollow form with empty hands."

And shall I take a thing so blind,
   Embrace her as my natural good;
   Or crush her, like a vice of blood,
Upon the threshold of the mind?

IV

To Sleep I give my powers away;
   My will is bondsman to the dark;
   I sit within a helmless bark,
And with my heart I muse and say:

O heart, how fares it with thee now,
   That thou should fail from thy desire,
   Who scarcely darest to inquire,
"What is it makes me beat so low?"

Something it is which thou hast lost,
   Some pleasure from thine early years.
   Break thou deep vase of chilling tears,
That grief hath shaken into frost!

Such clouds of nameless trouble cross
   All night below the darkened eyes;
   With morning wakes the will, and cries,
"Thou shalt not be the fool of loss."

V

I sometimes hold it half a sin
   To put in words the grief I feel;
   For words, like Nature, half reveal
And half conceal the Soul within.

But for the unquiet heart and brain
   A use in measured language lies;
   The sad mechanic exercise
Like dull narcotics numbing pain.

In words, like weeds, I'll wrap me o'er,
   Like coarsest clothes against the cold:
   But that large grief which these enfold
Is given in outline and no more.

VI

One writes, that "Other friends remain,"
   That "Loss is common to the race"—
   And common is the commonplace,
And vacant chaff well meant for grain.

That loss is common would not make
   My own less bitter, rather more:
   Too common! Never morning wore
To evening, but some heart did break.

O father, wheresoe'er thou be,
   Who pledgest now thy gallant son;
   A shot, ere half thy draught be done,
Hath still'd the life that beat from thee.

O mother, praying God will save
   Thy sailor,—while thy head is bow'd,
   His heavy-shotted hammock-shroud
Drops in his vast and wandering grave.

Ye know no more than I who wrought
   At that last hour to please him well;
   Who mused on all I had to tell,
And something written, something thought;

Expecting still his advent home;
   And ever met him on his way
   With wishes, thinking, "here to-day,"
Or "here to-morrow will he come."

O somewhere, meek, unconscious dove,
   That sittest ranging golden hair;
   And glad to find thyself so fair,
Poor child, that waitest for thy love!

For now her father's chimney glows
   In expectation of a guest;
   And thinking "this will please him best,"
She takes a riband or a rose;

For he will see them on to-night;
   And with the thought her colour burns;
   And, having left the glass, she turns
Once more to set a ringlet right;

And, even when she turn'd, the curse
   Had fallen, and her future Lord
   Was drown'd in passing thro' the ford,
Or kill'd in falling from his horse.

O what to her shall be the end?
   And what to me remains of good?
   To her, perpetual maidenhood,
And unto me no second friend.

VII

Dark house, by which once more I stand
   Here in the long unlovely street,
   Doors, where my heart was used to beat
So quickly, waiting for a hand,

A hand that can be clasp'd no more—
   Behold me, for I cannot sleep,
   And like a guilty thing I creep
At earliest morning to the door.

He is not here; but far away
   The noise of life begins again,
   And ghastly thro' the drizzling rain
On the bald street breaks the blank day.

VIII

A happy lover who has come
   To look on her that loves him well,
   Who 'lights and rings the gateway bell,
And learns her gone and far from home;

He saddens, all the magic light
   Dies off at once from bower and hall,
   And all the place is dark, and all
The chambers emptied of delight: <

So find I every pleasant spot
   In which we two were wont to meet,
   The field, the chamber, and the street,
For all is dark where thou art not.

Yet as that other, wandering there
   In those deserted walks, may find
   A flower beat with rain and wind,
Which once she fostered up with care;

So seems it in my deep regret,
   O my forsaken heart, with thee
   And this poor flower of poesy
Which little cared for fades not yet.

But since it pleased a vanish'd eye,
   I go to plant it on his tomb,
   That if it can it there may bloom,
Or, dying, there at least may die.

IX

Fair ship, that from the Italian shore
   Sailest the placid ocean-plains
   With my lost Arthur's loved remains,
Spread thy full wings, and waft him o'er.

So draw him home to those that mourn
   In vain; a favourable speed
   Ruffle thy mirror'd mast, and lead
Thro' prosperous floods his holy urn.

All night no ruder air perplex
   Thy sliding keel, till Phosphor, bright
   As our pure love, thro' early light
Shall glimmer on the dewy decks.

Sphere all your lights around, above;
   Sleep, gentle heavens, before the prow;
   Sleep, gentle winds, as he sleeps now,
My friend, the brother of my love;

My Arthur, whom I shall not see
   Till all my widow'd race be run;
   Dear as the mother to the son,
More than my brothers are to me.

X

I hear the noise about thy keel;
   I hear the bell struck in the night:
   I see the cabin-window bright;
I see the sailor at the wheel.

Thou bring'st the sailor to his wife,
   And travell'd men from foreign lands;
   And letters unto trembling hands;
And, thy dark freight, a vanish'd life.

So bring him; we have idle dreams:
   This look of quiet flatters thus
   Our home-bred fancies. O to us,
The fools of habit, sweeter seems

To rest beneath the clover sod,
   That takes the sunshine and the rains,
   Or where the kneeling hamlet drains
The chalice of the grapes of God;

Than if with thee the roaring wells
   Should gulf him fathom-deep in brine;
   And hands so often clasp'd in mine,
Should toss with tangle and with shells.

XI

Calm is the morn without a sound,
   Calm as to suit a calmer grief,
   And only thro' the faded leaf
The chestnut pattering to the ground:

Calm and deep peace on this high wold,
   And on these dews that drench the furze,
   And all the silvery gossamers
That twinkle into green and gold:

Calm and still light on yon great plain
  That sweeps with all its autumn bowers,
  And crowded farms and lessening towers,
To mingle with the bounding main:

Calm and deep peace in this wide air,
  These leaves that redden to the fall;
  And in my heart, if calm at all,
If any calm, a calm despair:

Calm on the seas, and silver sleep,
  And waves that sway themselves in rest,
  And dead calm in that noble breast
Which heaves but with the heaving deep.

XII

Lo, as a dove when up she springs
  To bear thro' Heaven a tale of woe,
  Some dolorous message knit below
The wild pulsation of her wings;

Like her I go; I cannot stay;
  I leave this mortal ark behind,
  A weight of nerves without a mind,
And leave the cliffs, and haste away

O'er ocean-mirrors rounded large,
  And reach the glow of southern skies,
  And see the sails at distance rise,
And linger weeping on the marge,

And saying; "Comes he thus, my friend?
  Is this the end of all my care?"
  And circle moaning in the air:
"Is this the end? Is this the end?"

And forward dart again, and play
  About the prow, and back return
  To where the body sits, and learn
That I have been an hour away.

XIII

Tears of the widower, when he sees
    A late-lost form that sleep reveals,
    And moves his doubtful arms, and feels
Her place is empty, fall like these;

Which weep a loss for ever new,
    A void where heart on heart reposed;
    And, where warm hands have prest and closed,
Silence, till I be silent too.

Which weep the comrade of my choice,
    An awful thought, a life removed,
    The human-hearted man I loved,
A Spirit, not a breathing voice.

Come, Time, and teach me, many years,
    I do not suffer in a dream;
    For now so strange do these things seem,
Mine eyes have leisure for their tears;

My fancies time to rise on wing,
    And glance about the approaching sails,
    As tho' they brought but merchants' bales,
And not the burthen that they bring.

XIV

If one should bring me this report,
    That thou hadst touch'd the land to-day,
    And I went down unto the quay,
And found thee lying in the port;

And standing, muffled round with woe,
    Should see thy passengers in rank
    Come stepping lightly down the plank,
And beckoning unto those they know;

And if along with these should come
    The man I held as half-divine;
    Should strike a sudden hand in mine,
And ask a thousand things of home;

And I should tell him all my pain,
   And how my life had droop'd of late,
   And he should sorrow o'er my state
And marvel what possess'd my brain;

And I perceived no touch of change,
   No hint of death in all his frame,
   But found him all in all the same,
I should not feel it to be strange.

XV

To-night the winds begin to rise
   And roar from yonder dropping day:
   The last red leaf is whirl'd away,
The rooks are blown about the skies;

The forest crack'd, the waters curl'd,
   The cattle huddled on the lea;
   And wildly dash'd on tower and tree
The sunbeam strikes along the world:

And but for fancies, which aver
   That all thy motions gently pass
   Athwart a plane of molten glass,
I scarce could brook the strain and stir

That makes the barren branches loud;
   And but for fear it is not so,
   The wild unrest that lives in woe
Would dote and pore on yonder cloud

That rises upward always higher,
   And onward drags a labouring breast,
   And topples round the dreary west,
A looming bastion fringed with fire.

XVI

What words are these have fall'n from me?
   Can calm despair and wild unrest
   Be tenants of a single breast,
Or sorrow such a changeling be?

Or doth she only seem to take
      The touch of change in calm or storm;
      But knows no more of transient form
   In her deep self, than some dead lake

   That holds the shadow of a lark
      Hung in the shadow of a heaven?
      Or has the shock, so harshly given,
   Confused me like the unhappy bark

   That strikes by night a craggy shelf,
      And staggers blindly ere she sink?
      And stunn'd me from my power to think
   And all my knowledge of myself;

   And made me that delirious man
      Whose fancy fuses old and new,
      And flashes into false and true,
   And mingles all without a plan?

XVII

   Thou comest, much wept for: such a breeze
      Compell'd thy canvas, and my prayer
      Was as the whisper of an air
   To breathe thee over lonely seas.

   For I in spirit saw thee move
      Thro' circles of the bounding sky,
      Week after week: the days go by:
   Come quick, thou bringest all I love.

   Henceforth, wherever thou may'st roam,
      My blessing, like a line of light,
      Is on the waters day and night,
   And like a beacon guards thee home.

   So may whatever tempest mars
      Mid-ocean, spare thee, sacred bark;
      And balmy drops in summer dark
   Slide from the bosom of the stars.

So kind an office hath been done,
  Such precious relics brought by thee;
  The dust of him I shall not see
Till all my widow'd race be run.

XVIII

'Tis well; 'tis something; we may stand
  Where he in English earth is laid,
  And from his ashes may be made
The violet of his native land.

'Tis little; but it looks in truth
  As if the quiet bones were blest
  Among familiar names to rest
And in the places of his youth.

Come then, pure hands, and bear the head
  That sleeps or wears the mask of sleep,
  And come, whatever loves to weep,
And hear the ritual of the dead.

Ah yet, ev'n yet, if this might be,
  I, falling on his faithful heart,
  Would breathing thro' his lips impart
The life that almost dies in me;

That dies not, but endures with pain,
  And slowly forms the firmer mind,
  Treasuring the look it cannot find,
The words that are not heard again.

XIX

The Danube to the Severn gave
  The darken'd heart that beat no more;
  They laid him by the pleasant shore,
And in the hearing of the wave.

There twice a day the Severn fills;
  The salt sea-water passes by,
  And hushes half the babbling Wye,
And makes a silence in the hills.

The Wye is hush'd nor moved along,
   And hush'd my deepest grief of all,
   When fill'd with tears that cannot fall,
I brim with sorrow drowning song.

The tide flows down, the wave again
   Is vocal in its wooded walls;
   My deeper anguish also falls,
And I can speak a little then.

XX

The lesser griefs that may be said,
   That breathe a thousand tender vows,
   Are but as servants in a house
Where lies the master newly dead;

Who speak their feeling as it is,
   And weep the fulness from the mind:
   "It will be hard," they say, "to find
Another service such as this."

My lighter moods are like to these,
   That out of words a comfort win;
   But there are other griefs within,
And tears that at their fountain freeze;

For by the hearth the children sit
   Cold in that atmosphere of Death,
   And scarce endure to draw the breath,
Or like to noiseless phantoms flit;

But open converse is there none,
   So much the vital spirits sink
   To see the vacant chair, and think,
"How good! how kind! and he is gone."

XXI

I sing to him that rests below,
   And, since the grasses round me wave,
   I take the grasses of the grave,
And make them pipes whereon to blow.

The traveller hears me now and then,
   And sometimes harshly will he speak:
   "This fellow would make weakness weak,
And melt the waxen hearts of men."

Another answers, "Let him be,
   He loves to make parade of pain
   That with his piping he may gain
The praise that comes to constancy."

A third is wroth: "Is this an hour
   For private sorrow's barren song,
   When more and more the people throng
The chairs and thrones of civil power?

"A time to sicken and to swoon,
   When Science reaches forth her arms
   To feel from world to world, and charms
Her secret from the latest moon?"

Behold, ye speak an idle thing:
   Ye never knew the sacred dust:
   I do but sing because I must,
And pipe but as the linnets sing:

And one is glad; her note is gay,
   For now her little ones have ranged;
   And one is sad; her note is changed,
Because her brood is stol'n away.

XXII

The path by which we twain did go,
   Which led by tracts that pleased us well,
   Thro' four sweet years arose and fell,
From flower to flower, from snow to snow:

And we with singing cheer'd the way,
   And, crown'd with all the season lent,
   From April on to April went,
And glad at heart from May to May:

But where the path we walk'd began
   To slant the fifth autumnal slope,
   As we descended following Hope,
There sat the Shadow fear'd of man;

Who broke our fair companionship,
   And spread his mantle dark and cold,
   And wrapt thee formless in the fold,
And dull'd the murmur on thy lip,

And bore thee where I could not see
   Nor follow, tho' I walk in haste,
   And think, that somewhere in the waste
The Shadow sits and waits for me.

XXIII

Now, sometimes in my sorrow shut,
   Or breaking into song by fits,
   Alone, alone, to where he sits,
The Shadow cloak'd from head to foot,

Who keeps the keys of all the creeds,
   I wander, often falling lame,
   And looking back to whence I came,
Or on to where the pathway leads;

And crying, How changed from where it ran
   Thro' lands where not a leaf was dumb;
   But all the lavish hills would hum
The murmur of a happy Pan:

When each by turns was guide to each,
   And Fancy light from Fancy caught,
   And Thought leapt out to wed with Thought
Ere Thought could wed itself with Speech;

And all we met was fair and good,
   And all was good that time could bring,
   And all the secret of the Spring
Moved in the chambers of the blood;

And many an old philosophy
   On Argive heights divinely sang,
   And round us all the thicket rang
To many a flute of Arcady.

XXIV

And was the day of my delight
   As pure and perfect as I say?
   The very source and fount of Day
Is dash'd with wandering isles of night.

If all was good and fair we met,
   This earth had been the Paradise
   It never look'd to human eyes
Since our first Sun arose and set.

And is it that the haze of grief
   Makes former gladness loom so great?
   The lowness of the present state,
That sets the past in this relief?

Or that the past will always win
   A glory from its being far;
   And orb into the perfect star
We saw not, when we moved therein?

XXV

I know that this was Life,—the track
   Whereon with equal feet we fared;
   And then, as now, the day prepared
The daily burden for the back.

But this it was that made me move
   As light as carrier-birds in air;
   I loved the weight I had to bear,
Because it needed help of Love:

Nor could I weary, heart or limb,
   When mighty Love would cleave in twain
   The lading of a single pain,
And part it, giving half to him.

XXVI

Still onward winds the dreary way;
   I with it; for I long to prove
   No lapse of moons can canker Love,
Whatever fickle tongues may say.

And if that eye which watches guilt
   And goodness, and hath power to see
   Within the green the moulder'd tree,
And towers fall'n as soon as built—

Oh, if indeed that eye foresee
   Or see (in Him is no before)
   In more of life true life no more
And Love the indifference to be,

Then might I find, ere yet the morn
   Breaks hither over Indian seas,
   That Shadow waiting with the keys,
To shroud me from my proper scorn.

XXVII

I envy not in any moods
   The captive void of noble rage,
   The linnet born within the cage,
That never knew the summer woods:

I envy not the beast that takes
   His license in the field of time,
   Unfetter'd by the sense of crime,
To whom a conscience never wakes;

Nor, what may count itself as blest,
   The heart that never plighted troth
   But stagnates in the weeds of sloth;
Nor any want-begotten rest.

I hold it true, whate'er befall;
   I feel it, when I sorrow most;
   'Tis better to have loved and lost
Than never to have loved at all.

XXVIII

The time draws near the birth of Christ:
   The moon is hid; the night is still;
   The Christmas bells from hill to hill
Answer each other in the mist.

Four voices of four hamlets round,
   From far and near, on mead and moor,
   Swell out and fail, as if a door
Were shut between me and the sound:

Each voice four changes on the wind,
   That now dilate, and now decrease,
   Peace and goodwill, goodwill and peace,
Peace and goodwill, to all mankind.

This year I slept and woke with pain,
   I almost wish'd no more to wake,
   And that my hold on life would break
Before I heard those bells again:

But they my troubled spirit rule,
   For they controll'd me when a boy;
   They bring me sorrow touch'd with joy,
The merry merry bells of Yule.

XXIX

With such compelling cause to grieve
   As daily vexes household peace,
   And chains regret to his decease,
How dare we keep our Christmas bells-eve;

Which brings no more a welcome guest
   To enrich the threshold of the night
   With shower'd largess of delight
In dance and song and game and jest?

Yet go, and while the holly boughs
   Entwine the cold baptismal font,
   Make one wreath more for Use and Wont,
That guard the portals of the house;

Old sisters of a day gone by,
  Gray nurses, loving nothing new;
  Why should they miss their yearly due
Before their time? They too will die.

XXX

With trembling fingers did we weave
  The holly round the Chrismas hearth;
  A rainy cloud possess'd the earth,
And sadly fell our Christmas bells-eve.

At our old pastimes in the hall
  We gambol'd, making vain pretence
  Of gladness, with an awful sense
Of one mute Shadow watching all.

We paused: the winds were in the beech
  We heard them sweep the winter land
  And in a circle hand-in-hand
Sat silent, looking each at each.

Then echo-like our voices rang;
  We sung, tho' every eye was dim,
  A merry song we sang with him
Last year: impetuously we sang:

We ceased: a gentler feeling crept
  Upon us: surely rest is meet:
  "They rest," we said, "their sleep is sweet,"
And silence follow'd, and we wept.

Our voices took a higher range;
  Once more we sang: "They do not die
  Nor lose their mortal sympathy,
Nor change to us, although they change;

"Rapt from the fickle and the frail
  With gather'd power, yet the same,
  Pierces the keen seraphic flame
From orb to orb, from veil to veil."

Rise, happy morn, rise, holy morn,
    Draw forth the cheerful day from night:
    O Father, touch the east, and light
The light that shone when Hope was born.

XXXI

When Lazarus left his charnel-cave,
    And home to Mary's house return'd,
    Was this demanded—if he yearn'd
To hear her weeping by his grave?

"Where wert thou, brother, those four days?"
    There lives no record of reply,
    Which telling what it is to die
Had surely added praise to praise.

From every house the neighbours met,
    The streets were fill'd with joyful sound,
    A solemn gladness even crown'd
The purple brows of Olivet.

Behold a man raised up by Christ!
    The rest remaineth unreveal'd;
    He told it not; or something seal'd
The lips of that Evangelist.

XXXII

Her eyes are homes of silent prayer,
    Nor other thought her mind admits
    But, he was dead, and there he sits,
And he that brought him back is there.

Then one deep love doth supersede
    All other, when her ardent gaze
    Roves from the living brother's face,
And rests upon the Life indeed.

All subtle thought, all curious fears,
    Borne down by gladness so complete,
    She bows, she bathes the Saviour's feet
With costly spikenard and with tears.

Thrice blest whose lives are faithful prayers,
   Whose loves in higher love endure;
   What souls possess themselves so pure,
Or is there blessedness like theirs?

XXXIII

O thou that after toil and storm
   Mayst seem to have reach'd a purer air,
   Whose faith has centre everywhere,
Nor cares to fix itself to form,

Leave thou thy sister when she prays,
   Her early Heaven, her happy views;
   Nor thou with shadow'd hint confuse
A life that leads melodious days.

Her faith thro' form is pure as thine,
   Her hands are quicker unto good:
   Oh, sacred be the flesh and blood
To which she links a truth divine!

See thou, that countest reason ripe
   In holding by the law within,
   Thou fail not in a world of sin,
And ev'n for want of such a type.

XXXIV

My own dim life should teach me this,
   That life shall live for evermore,
   Else earth is darkness at the core,
And dust and ashes all that is;

This round of green, this orb of flame,
   Fantastic beauty; such as lurks
   In some wild Poet, when he works
Without a conscience or an aim.

What then were God to such as I?
   'Twere hardly worth my while to choose
   Of things all mortal, or to use
A tattle patience ere I die;

'Twere best at once to sink to peace,
   Like birds the charming serpent draws,
   To drop head-foremost in the jaws
Of vacant darkness and to cease.

XXXV

Yet if some voice that man could trust
   Should murmur from the narrow house,
   "The cheeks drop in; the body bows;
Man dies: nor is there hope in dust:"

Might I not say? "Yet even here,
   But for one hour, O Love, I strive
   To keep so sweet a thing alive."
But I should turn mine ears and hear

The moanings of the homeless sea,
   The sound of streams that swift or slow
   Draw down Aeonian hills, and sow
The dust of continents to be;

And Love would answer with a sigh,
   "The sound of that forgetful shore
   Will change my sweetness more and more,
Half-dead to know that I shall die."

O me, what profits it to put
   An idle case? If Death were seen
   At first as Death, Love had not been,
Or been in narrowest working shut,

Mere fellowship of sluggish moods,
   Or in his coarsest Satyr-shape
   Had bruised the herb and crush'd the grape,
And bask'd and batten'd in the woods.

XXXVI

Tho' truths in manhood darkly join,
   Deep-seated in our mystic frame,
   We yield all blessing to the name
Of Him that made them current coin;

For Wisdom dealt with mortal powers,
   Where truth in closest words shall fail,
   When truth embodied in a tale
Shall enter in at lowly doors.

And so the Word had breath, and wrought
   With human hands the creed of creeds
   In loveliness of perfect deeds,
More strong than all poetic thought;

Which he may read that binds the sheaf,
   Or builds the house, or digs the grave,
   And those wild eyes that watch the wave
In roarings round the coral reef.

XXXVII

Urania speaks with darken'd brow:
   "Thou pratest here where thou art least;
   This faith has many a purer priest,
And many an abler voice than thou.

"Go down beside thy native rill,
   On thy Parnassus set thy feet,
   And hear thy laurel whisper sweet
About the ledges of the hill."

And my Melpomene replies,
   A touch of shame upon her cheek:
   "I am not worthy ev'n to speak
Of thy prevailing mysteries;

"For I am but an earthly Muse,
   And owning but a little art
   To lull with song an aching heart,
And render human love his dues;

"But brooding on the dear one dead,
   And all he said of things divine,
   (And dear to me as sacred wine
To dying lips is all he said),

"I murmur'd, as I came along,
   Of comfort clasp'd in truth reveal'd;
   And loiter'd in the master's field,
And darken'd sanctities with song."

XXXVIII

With weary steps I loiter on,
   Tho' always under alter'd skies
   The purple from the distance dies,
My prospect and horizon gone.

No joy the blowing season gives,
   The herald melodies of spring,
   But in the songs I love to sing
A doubtful gleam of solace lives.

If any care for what is here
   Survive in spirits render'd free,
   Then are these songs I sing of thee
Not all ungrateful to thine ear.

XXXIX

Old warder of these buried bones,
   And answering now my random stroke
   With fruitful cloud and living smoke,
Dark yew, that graspest at the stones

And dippest toward the dreamless head,
   To thee too comes the golden hour
   When flower is feeling after flower;
But Sorrow—fixt upon the dead,

And darkening the dark graves of men,—
   What whisper'd from her lying lips?
   Thy gloom is kindled at the tips,
And passes into gloom again.

XL

Could we forget the widow'd hour
   And look on Spirits breathed away,
   As on a maiden in the day
When first she wears her orange-flower!

When crown'd with blessing she doth rise
   To take her latest leave of home,
   And hopes and light regrets that come
Make April of her tender eyes;

And doubtful joys the father move,
   And tears are on the mother's face,
   As parting with a long embrace
She enters other realms of love;

Her office there to rear, to teach,
   Becoming as is meet and fit
   A link among the days, to knit
The generations each with each;

And, doubtless, unto thee is given
   A life that bears immortal fruit
   In those great offices that suit
The full-grown energies of heaven.

Ay me, the difference I discern!
   How often shall her old fireside
   Be cheer'd with tidings of the bride,
How often she herself return,

And tell them all they would have told,
   And bring her babe, and make her boast,
   Till even those that miss'd her most
Shall count new things as dear as old:

But thou and I have shaken hands,
   Till growing winters lay me low;
   My paths are in the fields I know.
And thine in undiscover'd lands.

XLI

Thy spirit ere our fatal loss
   Did ever rise from high to higher;
   As mounts the heavenward altar-fire,
As flies the lighter thro' the gross.

But thou art turn'd to something strange,
   And I have lost the links that bound
   Thy changes; here upon the ground,
No more partaker of thy change.

Deep folly! yet that this could be—
   That I could wing my will with might
   To leap the grades of life and light,
And flash at once, my friend, to thee.

For tho' my nature rarely yields
   To that vague fear implied in death;
   Nor shudders at the gulfs beneath,
The howlings from forgotten fields;

Yet oft when sundown skirts the moor
   An inner trouble I behold,
   A spectral doubt which makes me cold,
That I shall be thy mate no more,

Tho' following with an upward mind
   The wonders that have come to thee,
   Thro' all the secular to-be,
But evermore a life behind.

XLII

I vex my heart with fancies dim:
   He still outstript me in the race;
   It was but unity of place
That made me dream I rank'd with him.

And so may Place retain us still,
   And he the much-beloved again,
   A lord of large experience, train
To riper growth the mind and will:

And what delights can equal those
   That stir the spirit's inner deeps,
   When one that loves but knows not, reaps
A truth from one that loves and knows?

XLIII

If Sleep and Death be truly one,
   And every spirit's folded bloom
   Thro' all its intervital gloom
In some long trance should slumber on;

Unconscious of the sliding hour,
   Bare of the body, might it last,
   And silent traces of the past
Be all the colour of the flower:

So then were nothing lost to man;
   So that still garden of the souls
   In many a figured leaf enrolls
The total world since life began;

And love will last as pure and whole
   As when he loved me here in Time,
   And at the spiritual prime
Rewaken with the dawning soul.

XLIV

How fares it with the happy dead?
   For here the man is more and more;
   But he forgets the days before
God shut the doorways of his head.

The days have vanish'd, tone and tint,
   And yet perhaps the hoarding sense
   Gives out at times (he knows not whence)
A little flash, a mystic hint;

And in the long harmonious years
   (If Death so taste Lethean springs),
   May some dim touch of earthly things
Surprise thee ranging with thy peers.

If such a dreamy touch should fall,
   O, turn thee round, resolve the doubt;
   My guardian angel will speak out
In that high place, and tell thee all.

XLV

The baby new to earth and sky,
   What time his tender palm is prest
   Against the circle of the breast,
Has never thought that "this is I:"

But as he grows he gathers much,
   And learns the use of "I," and "me,"
   And finds "I am not what I see,
And other than the things I touch."

So rounds he to a separate mind
   From whence clear memory may begin,
   As thro' the frame that binds him in
His isolation grows defined.

This use may lie in blood and breath,
   Which else were fruitless of their due,
   Had man to learn himself anew
Beyond the second birth of Death.

XLVI

We ranging down this lower track,
   The path we came by, thorn and flower,
   Is shadow'd by the growing hour,
Lest life should fail in looking back.

So be it: there no shade can last
   In that deep dawn behind the tomb,
   But clear from marge to marge shall bloom
The eternal landscape of the past;

A lifelong tract of time reveal'd;
   The fruitful hours of still increase;
   Days order'd in a wealthy peace,
And those five years its richest field.

O Love, thy province were not large,
   A bounded field, nor stretching far;
   Look also, Love, a brooding star,
A rosy warmth from marge to marge.

XLVII

That each, who seems a separate whole,
   Should move his rounds, and fusing all
   The skirts of self again, should fall
Remerging in the general Soul,

Is faith as vague as all unsweet:
   Eternal form shall still divide
   The eternal soul from all beside;
And I shall know him when we meet:

And we shall sit at endless feast,
   Enjoying each the other's good:
   What vaster dream can hit the mood
Of Love on earth? He seeks at least

Upon the last and sharpest height,
   Before the spirits fade away,
   Some landing-place, to clasp and say,
"Farewell! We lose ourselves in light."

XLVIII

If these brief lays, of Sorrow born,
   Were taken to be such as closed
   Grave doubts and answers here proposed,
Then these were such as men might scorn:

Her care is not to part and prove;
   She takes, when harsher moods remit,
   What slender shade of doubt may flit,
And makes it vassal unto love:

And hence, indeed, she sports with words,
   But better serves a wholesome law,
   And holds it sin and shame to draw
The deepest measure from the chords:

    Nor dare she trust a larger lay,
        But rather loosens from the lip
        Short swallow-flights of song, that dip
    Their wings in tears, and skim away.

XLIX

From art, from nature, from the schools,
    Let random influences glance,
    Like light in many a shiver'd lance
That breaks about the dappled pools:

The lightest wave of thought shall lisp,
    The fancy's tenderest eddy wreathe,
    The slightest air of song shall breathe
To make the sullen surface crisp.

And look thy look, and go thy way,
    But blame not thou the winds that make
    The seeming-wanton ripple break,
The tender-pencil'd shadow play.

Beneath all fancied hopes and fears
    Ay me, the sorrow deepens down,
    Whose muffled motions blindly drown
The bases of my life in tears.

L

Be near me when my light is low,
    When the blood creeps, and the nerves prick
    And tingle; and the heart is sick,
And all the wheels of Being slow.

Be near me when the sensuous frame
    Is rack'd with pangs that conquer trust;
    And Time, a maniac scattering dust,
And Life, a Fury slinging flame.

Be near me when my faith is dry,
    And men the flies of latter spring,
    That lay their eggs, and sting and sing
And weave their petty cells and die.

Be near me when I fade away,
  To point the term of human strife,
  And on the low dark verge of life
The twilight of eternal day.

LI

Do we indeed desire the dead
  Should still be near us at our side?
  Is there no baseness we would hide?
No inner vileness that we dread?

Shall he for whose applause I strove,
  I had such reverence for his blame,
  See with clear eye some hidden shame
And I be lessen'd in his love?

I wrong the grave with fears untrue:
  Shall love be blamed for want of faith?
  There must be wisdom with great Death:
The dead shall look me thro' and thro'.

Be near us when we climb or fall:
  Ye watch, like God, the rolling hours
  With larger other eyes than ours,
To make allowance for us all.

LII

I cannot love thee as I ought,
  For love reflects the thing beloved;
  My words are only words, and moved
Upon the topmost froth of thought.

"Yet blame not thou thy plaintive,"
  The Spirit of true love replied;
  "Thou canst not move me from thy side,
Nor human frailty do me wrong.

"What keeps a spirit wholly true
  To that ideal which he bears?
  What record? not the sinless years
That breathed beneath the Syrian blue:

"So fret not, like an idle girl,
   That life is dash'd with flecks of sin.
   Abide: thy wealth is gather'd in,
When time hath sunder'd shell from pearl."

LIII

How many a father have I seen,
   A sober man, among his boys,
   Whose youth was full of foolish noise,
Who wears his manhood hale and green:

And dare we to this fancy give,
   That had the wild oat not been sown,
   The soil, left barren, scarce had grown
The grain by which a man may live?

Or, if we held the doctrine sound
   For life outliving heats of youth,
   Yet who would preach it as a truth
To those that eddy round and round?

Hold thou the good: define it well:
   For fear divine Philosophy
   Should push beyond her mark, and be
Procuress to the Lords of Hell.

LIV

Oh, yet we trust that somehow good
   Will be the final goal of ill,
   To pangs of nature, sins of will,
Defects of doubt, and taints of blood;

That nothing walks with aimless feet;
   That not one life shall be destroy'd,
   Or cast as rubbish to the void,
When God hath made the pile complete;

That not a worm is cloven in vain;
   That not a moth with vain desire
   Is shrivell'd in a fruitless fire,
Or but subserves another's gain.

Behold, we know not anything;
   I can but trust that good shall fall
   At last—far off—at last, to all,
And every winter change to spring.

So runs my dream: but what am I?
   An infant crying in the night:
   An infant crying for the light:
And with no language but a cry.

LV

The wish, that of the living whole
   No life may fail beyond the grave,
   Derives it not from what we have
The likest God within the soul?

Are God and Nature then at strife,
   That Nature lends such evil dreams?
   So careful of the type she seems,
So careless of the single life;

That I, considering everywhere
   Her secret meaning in her deeds,
   And finding that of fifty seeds
She often brings but one to bear,

I falter where I firmly trod,
   And falling with my weight of cares
   Upon the great world's altar-stairs
That slope thro' darkness up to God,

I stretch lame hands of faith, and grope,
   And gather dust and chaff, and call
   To what I feel is Lord of all,
And faintly trust the larger hope.

LVI

"So careful of the type?" but no.
   From scarped cliff and quarried stone
   She cries, "A thousand types are gone:
I care for nothing, all shall go.

"Thou makest thine appeal to me:
   I bring to life, I bring to death:
   The spirit does but mean the breath:
I know no more." And he, shall he,

Man, her last work, who seem'd so fair,
   Such splendid purpose in his eyes,
   Who roll'd the psalm to wintry skies,
Who built him fanes of fruitless prayer,

Who trusted God was love indeed
   And love Creation's final law—
   Tho' Nature, red in tooth and claw
With ravine, shriek'd against his creed—

Who loved, who suffer'd countless ills,
   Who battled for the True, the Just,
   Be blown about the desert dust,
Or seal'd within the iron hills?

No more? A monster then, a dream,
   A discord. Dragons of the prime,
   That tare each other in their slime,
Were mellow music match'd with him.

O life as futile, then, as frail!
   O for thy voice to soothe and bless!
   What hope of answer, or redress?
Behind the veil, behind the veil.

LVII

Peace; come away: the song of woe
   Is after all an earthly song:
   Peace; come away: we do him wrong
To sing so wildly: let us go.

Come; let us go: your cheeks are pale;
   But half my life I leave behind:
   Methinks my friend is richly shrined;
But I shall pass; my work will fail.

Yet in these ears, till hearing dies,
   One set slow bell will seem to toll
   The passing of the sweetest soul
That ever look'd with human eyes.

I hear it now, and o'er and o'er,
   Eternal greetings to the dead;
   And "Ave, Ave, Ave," said,
"Adieu, adieu," for evermore.

LVIII

In those sad words I took farewell:
   Like echoes in sepulchral halls,
   As drop by drop the water falls
In vaults and catacombs, they fell;

And, falling, idly broke the peace
   Of hearts that beat from day to day,
   Half-conscious of their dying clay,
And those cold crypts where they shall cease.

The high Muse answer'd: "Wherefore grieve
   Thy brethren with a fruitless tear?
   Abide a little longer here,
And thou shalt take a nobler leave."

LIX

O Sorrow, wilt thou live with me
   No casual mistress, but a wife,
   My bosom-friend and half of life;
As I confess it needs must be;

O Sorrow, wilt thou rule my blood,
   Be sometimes lovely like a bride,
   And put thy harsher moods aside,
If thou wilt have me wise and good.

My centred passion cannot move,
   Nor will it lessen from to-day;
   But I'll have leave at times to play
As with the creature of my love;

And set thee forth, for thou art mine,
   With so much hope for years to come,
   That, howsoe'er I know thee, some
Could hardly tell what name were thine.

LX

He past; a soul of nobler tone:
   My spirit loved and loves him yet,
   Like some poor girl whose heart is set
On one whose rank exceeds her own.

He mixing with his proper sphere,
   She finds the baseness of her lot,
   Half jealous of she knows not what,
And envying all that meet him there.

The little village looks forlorn;
   She sighs amid her narrow days,
   Moving about the household ways,
In that dark house where she was born.

The foolish neighbors come and go,
   And tease her till the day draws by:
   At night she weeps, "How vain am I!
How should he love a thing so low?"

LXI

If, in thy second state sublime,
   Thy ransom'd reason change replies
   With all the circle of the wise,
The perfect flower of human time;

And if thou cast thine eyes below,
   How dimly character'd and slight,
   How dwarf'd a growth of cold and night,
How blanch'd with darkness must I grow!

Yet turn thee to the doubtful shore,
   Where thy first form was made a man;
   I loved thee, Spirit, and love, nor can
The soul of Shakspeare love thee more.

LXII

Tho' if an eye that's downward cast
   Could make thee somewhat blench or fail,
   Then be my love an idle tale,
And fading legend of the past;

And thou, as one that once declined,
   When he was little more than boy,
   On some unworthy heart with joy,
But lives to wed an equal mind;

And breathes a novel world, the while
   His other passion wholly dies,
   Or in the light of deeper eyes
Is matter for a flying smile.

LXIII

Yet pity for a horse o'er-driven,
   And love in which my hound has part,
   Can hang no weight upon my heart
In its assumptions up to heaven;

And I am so much more than these,
   As thou, perchance, art more than I,
   And yet I spare them sympathy,
And I would set their pains at ease.

So mayst thou watch me where I weep,
   As, unto vaster motions bound,
   The circuits of thine orbit round
A higher height, a deeper deep.

LXIV

Dost thou look back on what hath been,
   As some divinely gifted man,
   Whose life in low estate began
And on a simple village green;

Who breaks his birth's invidious bar,
   And grasps the skirts of happy chance,
   And breasts the blows of circumstance,
And grapples with his evil star;

Who makes by force his merit known
   And lives to clutch the golden keys,
   To mould a mighty state's decrees,
And shape the whisper of the throne;

And moving up from high to higher,
   Becomes on Fortune's crowning slope
   The pillar of a people's hope,
The centre of a world's desire;

Yet feels, as in a pensive dream,
   When all his active powers are still,
   A distant dearness in the hill,
A secret sweetness in the stream,

The limit of his narrower fate,
   While yet beside its vocal springs
   He play'd at counsellors and kings,
With one that was his earliest mate;

Who ploughs with pain his native lea
   And reaps the labour of his hands,
   Or in the furrow musing stands;
"Does my old friend remember me?"

LXV

Sweet soul, do with me as thou wilt;
   I lull a fancy trouble-tost
   With "Love's too precious to be lost,
A little grain shall not be spilt."

And in that solace can I sing,
   Till out of painful phases wrought
   There flutters up a happy thought,
Self-balanced on a lightsome wing:

Since we deserved the name of friends,
   And thine effect so lives in me,
   A part of mine may live in thee
And move thee on to noble ends.

LXVI

You thought my heart too far diseased;
   You wonder when my fancies play
   To find me gay among the gay,
Like one with any trifle pleased.

The shade by which my life was crost,
   Which makes a desert in the mind,
   Has made me kindly with my kind,
And like to him whose sight is lost;

Whose feet are guided thro' the land,
   Whose jest among his friends is free,
   Who takes the children on his knee,
And winds their curls about his hand:

He plays with threads, he beats his chair
   For pastime, dreaming of the sky;
   His inner day can never die,
His night of loss is always there.

LXVII

When on my bed the moonlight falls,
   I know that in thy place of rest
   By that broad water of the west,
There comes a glory on the walls;

Thy marble bright in dark appears,
   As slowly steals a silver flame
   Along the letters of thy name,
And o'er the number of thy years.

The mystic glory swims away;
   From off my bed the moonlight dies;
   And closing eaves of wearied eyes
I sleep till dusk is dipt in gray;

And then I know the mist is drawn
   A lucid veil from coast to coast,
   And in the dark church like a ghost
Thy tablet glimmers to the dawn.

LXVIII

When in the down I sink my head,
   Sleep, Death's twin-brother, times my breath;
   Sleep, Death's twin-brother, knows not Death,
Nor can I dream of thee as dead:

I walk as ere I walk'd forlorn,
   When all our path was fresh with dew,
   And all the bugle breezes blew
Reveillée to the breaking morn.

But what is this? I turn about,
   I find a trouble in thine eye,
   Which makes me sad I know not why,
Nor can my dream resolve the doubt:

But ere the lark hath left the lea
   I wake, and I discern the truth;
   It is the trouble of my youth
That foolish sleep transfers to thee.

LXIX

I dream'd there would be Spring no more,
   That Nature's ancient power was lost:
   The streets were black with smoke and frost,
They chatter'd trifles at the door:

I wander'd from the noisy town,
   I found a wood with thorny boughs:
   I took the thorns to bind my brows,
I wore them like a civic crown:

I met with scoffs, I met with scorns
   From youth and babe and hoary hairs:
   They call'd me in the public squares
The fool that wears a crown of thorns:

They call'd me fool, they call'd me child:
   I found an angel of the night;
   The voice was low, the look was bright;
He look'd upon my crown and smiled:

He reach'd the glory of a hand,
   That seem'd to touch it into leaf:
   The voice was not the voice of grief,
The words were hard to understand.

LXX

I cannot see the features right,
   When on the gloom I strive to paint
   The face I know; the hues are faint
And mix with hollow masks of night;

Cloud-towers by ghostly masons wrought,
   A gulf that ever shuts and gapes,
   A hand that points, and palled shapes
In shadowy thoroughfares of thought;

And crowds that stream from yawning doors,
   And shoals of pucker'd faces drive;
   Dark bulks that tumble half alive,
And lazy lengths on boundless shores;

Till all at once beyond the will
   I hear a wizard music roll,
   And thro' a lattice on the soul
Looks thy fair face and makes it still.

LXXI

Sleep, kinsman thou to death and trance
   And madness, thou hast forged at last
   A night-long Present of the Past
In which we went thro' summer France.

Hadst thou such credit with the soul?
   Then bring an opiate trebly strong,
   Drug down the blindfold sense of wrong
That so my pleasure may be whole;

While now we talk as once we talk'd
    Of men and minds, the dust of change,
    The days that grow to something strange,
In walking as of old we walk'd

Beside the river's wooded reach,
    The fortress, and the mountain ridge,
    The cataract flashing from the bridge,
The breaker breaking on the beach.

LXXII

Risest thou thus, dim dawn, again,
    And howlest, issuing out of night,
    With blasts that blow the poplar white,
And lash with storm the streaming pane?

Day, when my crown'd estate begun
    To pine in that reverse of doom,
    Which sicken'd every living bloom,
And blurr'd the splendour of the sun;

Who usherest in the dolorous hour
    With thy quick tears that make the rose
    Pull sideways, and the daisy close
Her crimson fringes to the shower;

Who might'st have heaved a windless flame
    Up the deep East, or, whispering, play'd
    A chequer-work of beam and shade
Along the hills, yet look'd the same.

As wan, as chill, as wild as now;
    Day, mark'd as with some hideous crime,
    When the dark hand struck down thro' time,
And cancell'd nature's best: but thou,

Lift as thou may'st thy burthen'd brows
    Thro' clouds that drench the morning star,
    And whirl the ungarner'd sheaf afar,
And sow the sky with flying boughs,

And up thy vault with roaring sound
   Climb thy thick noon, disastrous day;
   Touch thy dull goal of joyless gray,
And hide thy shame beneath the ground.

LXXIII

So many worlds, so much to do,
   So little done, such things to be,
   How know I what had need of thee,
For thou wert strong as thou wert true?

The fame is quench'd that I foresaw,
   The head hath miss'd an earthly wreath:
   I curse not nature, no, nor death;
For nothing is that errs from law.

We pass; the path that each man trod
   Is dim, or will be dim, with weeds:
   What fame is left for human deeds
In endless age? It rests with God.

O hollow wraith of dying fame,
   Fade wholly, while the soul exults,
   And self-infolds the large results
Of force that would have forged a name.

LXXIV

As sometimes in a dead man's face,
   To those that watch it more and more,
   A likeness, hardly seen before,
Comes out—to some one of his race:

So, dearest, now thy brows are cold,
   I see thee what thou art, and know
   Thy likeness to the wise below,
Thy kindred with the great of old.

But there is more than I can see,
   And what I see I leave unsaid,
   Nor speak it, knowing Death has made
His darkness beautiful with thee.

I leave thy praises unexpress'd
   In verse that brings myself relief,
   And by the measure of my grief
I leave thy greatness to be guess'd;

What practice howsoe'er expert
   In fitting aptest words to things,
   Or voice the richest-toned that sings,
Hath power to give thee as thou wert?

I care not in these fading days
   To raise a cry that lasts not long,
   And round thee with the breeze of song
To stir a little dust of praise.

Thy leaf has perish'd in the green,
   And, while we breathe beneath the sun,
   The world which credits what is done
Is cold to all that might have been.

So here shall silence guard thy fame;
   But somewhere, out of human view,
   Whate'er thy hands are set to do
Is wrought with tumult of acclaim.

LXXV

I leave thy praises unexpress'd
   In verse that brings myself relief,
   And by the measure of my grief
I leave thy greatness to be guess'd;

What practice howsoe'er expert
   In fitting aptest words to things,
   Or voice the richest-toned that sings,
Hath power to give thee as thou wert?

I care not in these fading days
   To raise a cry that lasts not long,
   And round thee with the breeze of song
To stir a little dust of praise.

Thy leaf has perish'd in the green,
   And, while we breathe beneath the sun,
   The world which credits what is done
Is cold to all that might have been.

So here shall silence guard thy fame;
   But somewhere, out of human view,
   Whate'er thy hands are set to do
Is wrought with tumult of acclaim.

LXXVI

Take wings of fancy, and ascend,
   And in a moment set thy face
   Where all the starry heavens of space
Are sharpen'd to a needle's end;

Take wings of foresight; lighten thro'
   The secular abyss to come,
   And lo, thy deepest lays are dumb
Before the mouldering of a yew;

And if the matin songe, that woke
   The darkness of our planet, last,
   Thine own shall wither in the vast,
Ere half the lifetime of an oak.

Ere these have clothed their branchy bowers
   With fifty Mays, thy songs are vain;
   And what are they when these remain
The ruin'd shells of hollow towers?

LXXVII

What hope is here for modern rhyme
   To him, who turns a musing eye
   On songs, and deeds, and lives, that lie
Foreshorten'd in the tract of time?

These mortal lullabies of pain
   May bind a book, may line a box,
   May serve to curl a maiden's locks;
Or when a thousand moons shall wane

A man upon a stall may find,
    And, passing, turn the page that tells
    A grief, then changed to something else,
Sung by a long-forgotten mind.

But what of that? My darken'd ways
    Shall ring with music all the same;
    To breathe my loss is more than fame,
To utter love more sweet than praise.

LXXVIII

Again at Christmas bells did we weave
    The holly round the Christmas hearth;
    The silent snow possess'd the earth,
And calmly fell our Christmas-eve:

The yule-clog sparkled keen with frost,
    No wing of wind the region swept,
    But over all things brooding slept
The quiet sense of something lost.

As in the winters left behind,
    Again our ancient games had place,
    The mimic picture's breathing grace,
And dance and song and hoodman-blind.

Who show'd a token of distress?
    No single tear, no mark of pain:
    O sorrow, then can sorrow wane?
O grief, can grief be changed to less?

O last regret, regret can die!
    No—mixt with all this mystic frame,
    Her deep relations are the same,
But with long use her tears are dry.

LXXIX

"More than my brothers are to me,"—
    Let this not vex thee, noble heart!
    I know thee of what force thou art
To hold the costliest love in fee.

But thou and I are one in kind,
    As moulded like in Nature's mint;
    And hill and wood and field did print
The same sweet forms in either mind.

For us the same cold streamlet curl'd
    Thro' all his eddying coves, the same
    All winds that roam the twilight came
In whispers of the beauteous world.

At one dear knee we proffer'd vows,
    One lesson from one book we learn'd,
    Ere childhood's flaxen ringlet turn'd
To black and brown on kindred brows.

And so my wealth resembles thine,
    But he was rich where I was poor,
    And he supplied my want the more
As his unlikeness fitted mine.

LXXX

If any vague desire should rise,
    That holy Death ere Arthur died
    Had moved me kindly from his side,
And dropt the dust on tearlesss eyes;

Then fancy shapes, as fancy can,
    The grief my loss in him had wrought,
    A grief as deep as life or thought,
But stay'd in peace with God and man.

I make a picture in the brain;
    I hear the sentence that he speaks;
    He bears the burthen of the weeks
But turns his burthen into gain.

His credit thus shall set me free;
    And, influence-rich to soothe and save,
    Unused example from the grave
Reach out dead hands to comfort me.

LXXXI

Could I have said while he was here,
   "My love shall now no further range;
   There cannot come a mellower change,
For now is love mature in ear"?

Love, then, had hope of richer store:
   What end is here to my complaint?
   This haunting whisper makes me faint,
"More years had made me love thee more.'

But Death returns an answer sweet:
   "My sudden frost was sudden gain,
   And gave all ripeness to the grain,
It might have drawn from after-heat."

LXXXII

I wage not any feud with Death
   For changes wrought on form and face;
   No lower life that earth's embrace
May breed with him, can fright my faith.

Eternal process moving on,
   From state to state the spirit walks;
   And these are but the shatter'd stalks,
Or ruin'd chrysalis of one.

Nor blame I Death, because he bare
   The use of virtue out of earth:
   I know transplanted human worth
Will bloom to profit, otherwhere.

For this alone on Death I wreak
   The wrath that garners in my heart;
   He put our lives so far apart
We cannot hear each other speak.

LXXXIII

Dip down upon the northern shore,
   O sweet new-year delaying long;
   Thou doest expectant nature wrong;
Delaying long, delay no more.

What stays thee from the clouded noons,
   Thy sweetness from its proper place?
   Can trouble live with April days,
Or sadness in the summer moons?

Bring orchis, bring the foxglove spire,
   The little speedwell's darling blue,
   Deep tulips dash'd with fiery dew,
Laburnums, dropping-wells of fire.

O thou, new-year, delaying long,
   Delayest the sorrow in my blood,
   That longs to burst a frozen bud
And flood a fresher throat with song.

LXXXIV

When I contemplate all alone
   The life that had been thine below,
   And fix my thoughts on all the glow
To which thy crescent would have grown;

I see thee sitting crown'd with good,
   A central warmth diffusing bliss
   In glance and smile, and clasp and kiss,
On all the branches of thy blood;

Thy blood, my friend, and partly mine;
   For now the day was drawing on,
   When thou should'st link thy life with one
Of mine own house, and boys of thine

Had babbled "Uncle" on my knee;
   But that remorseless iron hour
   Made cypress of her orange flower,
Despair of Hope, and earth of thee.

I seem to meet their least desire,
   To clap their cheeks, to call them mine.
   I see their unborn faces shine
Beside the never-lighted fire.

I see myself an honor'd guest,
   Thy partner in the flowery walk
   Of letters, genial table-talk,
Or deep dispute, and graceful jest;

While now thy prosperous labor fills
   The lips of men with honest praise,
   And sun by sun the happy days
Descend below the golden hills

With promise of a morn as fair,
   And all the train of bounteous hours
   Conduct by paths of growing powers,
To reverence and the silver hair;

Till slowly worn her earthly robe,
   Her lavish mission richly wrought,
   Leaving great legacies of thought,
Thy spirit should fail from off the globe;

What time mine own might also flee,
   As link'd with thine in love and fate,
   And, hovering o'er the dolorous strait
To the other shore, involved in thee,

Arrive at last the blessed goal,
   And He that died in Holy Land
   Would reach us out the shining hand,
And take us as a single soul.

What reed was that on which I leant?
   Ah, backward fancy, wherefore wake
   The old bitterness again, and break
The low beginnings of content.

LXXXV

This truth came borne with bier and pall
   I felt it, when I sorrow'd most,
   'Tis better to have loved and lost,
Than never to have loved at all—

O true in word, and tried in deed,
   Demanding, so to bring relief
   To this which is our common grief,
What kind of life is that I lead;

And whether trust in things above
   Be dimm'd of sorrow, or sustain'd;
   And whether love for him have drain'd
My capabilities of love;

Your words have virtue such as draws
   A faithful answer from the breast,
   Thro' light reproaches, half exprest,
And loyal unto kindly laws.

My blood an even tenor kept,
   Till on mine ear this message falls,
   That in Vienna's fatal walls
God's finger touch'd him, and he slept.

The great Intelligences fair
   That range above our mortal state,
   In circle round the blessed gate,
Received and gave him welcome there;

And led him thro' the blissful climes,
   And show'd him in the fountain fresh
   All knowledge that the sons of flesh
Shall gather in the cycled times.

But I remain'd, whose hopes were dim,
   Whose life, whose thoughts were little worth,
   To wander on a darken'd earth,
Where all things round me breathed of him.

Lord Alfred Tennyson

O friendship, equal-poised control,
   O heart, with kindliest motion warm,
   O sacred essence, other form,
O solemn ghost, O crowned soul!

Yet none could better know than I,
   How much of act at human hands
   The sense of human will demands
By which we dare to live or die.

Whatever way my days decline,
   I felt and feel, tho' left alone,
   His being working in mine own,
The footsteps of his life in mine;

A life that all the Muses deck'd
   With gifts of grace, that might express
   All-comprehensive tenderness,
All-subtilising intellect:

And so my passion hath not swerved
   To works of weakness, but I find
   An image comforting the mind,
And in my grief a strength reserved.

Likewise the imaginative woe,
   That loved to handle spiritual strife
   Diffused the shock thro' all my life,
But in the present broke the blow.

My pulses therefore beat again
   For other friends that once I met;
   Nor can it suit me to forget
The mighty hopes that make us men.

I woo your love: I count it crime
   To mourn for any overmuch;
   I, the divided half of such
A friendship as had master'd Time;

Which masters Time indeed, and is
   Eternal, separate from fears:
   The all-assuming months and years
Can take no part away from this:

But Summer on the steaming floods,
   And Spring that swells the narrow brooks,
   And Autumn, with a noise of rooks,
That gather in the waning woods,

And every pulse of wind and wave
   Recalls, in change of light or gloom,
   My old affection of the tomb,
And my prime passion in the grave:

My old affection of the tomb,
   A part of stillness, yearns to speak:
   "Arise, and get thee forth and seek
A friendship for the years to come.

"I watch thee from the quiet shore;
   Thy spirit up to mine can reach;
   But in dear words of human speech
We two communicate no more."

And I, "Can clouds of nature stain
   The starry clearness of the free?
   How is it? Canst thou feel for me
Some painless sympathy with pain?"

And lightly does the whisper fall:
   "'Tis hard for thee to fathom this;
   I triumph in conclusive bliss,
And that serene result of all."

So hold I commerce with the dead;
   Or so methinks the dead would say;
   Or so shall grief with symbols play
And pining life be fancy-fed.

Now looking to some settled end,
   That these things pass, and I shall prove
   A meeting somewhere, love with love,
I crave your pardon, O my friend;

If not so fresh, with love as true,
   I, clasping brother-hands, aver
   I could not, if I would, transfer
The whole I felt for him to you.

For which be they that hold apart
   The promise of the golden hours?
   First love, first friendship, equal powers,
That marry with the virgin heart.

Still mine, that cannot but deplore,
   That beats within a lonely place,
   That yet remembers his embrace,
But at his footstep leaps no more,

My heart, tho' widow'd, may not rest
   Quite in the love of what is gone,
   But seeks to beat in time with one
That warms another living breast.

Ah, take the imperfect gift I bring,
   Knowing the primrose yet is dear,
   The primrose of the later year,
As not unlike to that of Spring.

LXXXVI

Sweet after showers, ambrosial air,
   That rollest from the gorgeous gloom
   Of evening over brake and bloom
And meadow, slowly breathing bare

The round of space, and rapt below
   Thro' all the dewy-tassell'd wood,
   And shadowimg down the horned flood
In ripples, fan my brows and blow

The fever from my cheek, and sigh
   The full new life that feeds thy breath
   Throughout my frame, till Doubt and Death,
Ill brethren, let the fancy fly

From belt to belt of crimson seas
   On leagues of odour streaming far,
   To where in yonder orient star
A hundred spirits whisper "Peace."

LXXXVII

I past beside the reverend walls
   In which of old I wore the gown;
   I roved at random thro' the town,
And saw the tumult of the halls;

And heard once more in college fanes
   The storm their high-built organs make,
   And thunder-music, rolling, shake
The prophet blazon'd on the panes;

And caught once more the distant shout,
   The measured pulse of racing oars
   Among the willows; paced the shores
And many a bridge, and all about

The same gray flats again, and felt
   The same, but not the same; and last
   Up that long walk of limes I past
To see the rooms in which he dwelt.

Another name was on the door:
   I linger'd; all within was noise
   Of songs, and clapping shand, and boys
That crash'd the glass and beat the floor;

Where once we held debate, a band
   Of youthful friends, on mind and art,
   And labour, and the changing mart,
And all the framework of the land;

When one would aim an arrow fair,
   But send it slackly from the string;
   And one would pierce an outer ring,
And one an inner, here and there;

And last the master-bowman, he,
   Would cleave the mark. A willing ear
   We lent him. Who, but hung to hear
The rapt oration flowing free

From point to point, with power and grace
   And music in the bounds of law,
   To those conclusions when we saw
The God within him light his face,

And seem to lift the form, and glow
   In azure orbits heavenly-wise;
   And over those ethereal eyes
The bar of Michael Angelo?

LXXXVIII

Wild bird, whose warble, liquid sweet,
   Rings Eden thro' the budded quicks,
   O tell me where the senses mix,
O tell me where the passions meet,

Whence radiate: fierce extremes employ
   Thy spirits in the darkening leaf,
   And in the midmost heart of grief
Thy passion clasps a secret joy:

And I—my harp would prelude woe—
   I cannot all command the strings;
   The glory of the sum of things
Will flash along the chords and go

LXXXIX

Witch-elms that counterchange the floor
   Of this flat lawn with dusk and bright;
   And thou, with all thy breadth and height
Of foliage, towering sycamore;

How often, hither wandering down,
   My Arthur found your shadows fair,
   And shook to all the liberal air
The dust and din and steam of town:

He brought an eye for all he saw;
   He mixt in all our simple sports;
   They pleased him, fresh from brawling courts
And dusty purlieus of the law.

O joy to him in this retreat,
　　Immantled in ambrosial dark,
　　To drink the cooler air, and mark
The landscape winking thro' the heat:

O sound to rout the brood of cares,
　　The sweep of scythe in morning dew,
　　The gust that round the garden flew,
And tumbled half the mellowing pears!

O bliss, when all in circle drawn
　　About him, heart and ear were fed
　　To hear him as he lay and read
The Tuscan poets on the lawn:

Or in the all-golden afternoon
　　A guest, or happy sister, sung,
　　Or here she brought the harp and flung
A ballad to the brightening moon:

Nor less it pleased in livelier moods,
　　Beyond the bounding hill to stray,
　　And break the livelong summer day
With banquet in the distant woods;

Whereat we glanced from theme to theme,
　　Discuss'd the books to love or hate,
　　Or touch'd the changes of the state,
Or threaded some Socratic dream;

But if I praised the busy town,
　　He loved to rail against it still,
　　For "ground in yonder social mill
We rub each other's angles down,

"And merge," he said, "in form and gloss
　　The picturesque of man and man."
　　We talk'd: the stream beneath us ran,
The wine-flask lying couch'd in moss,

Or cool'd within the glooming wave;
　　And last, returning from afar,
　　Before the crimson-circled star
Had fall'n into her father's grave,

And brushing ankle-deep in flowers,
   We heard behind the woodbine veil
   The milk that bubbled in the pail,
And buzzings of the honied hours.

XC

He tasted love with half his mind,
   Nor ever drank the inviolate spring
   Where nighest heaven, who first could fling
This bitter seed among mankind;

That could the dead, whose dying eyes
   Were closed with wail, resume their life,
   They would but find in child and wife
An iron welcome when they rise:

'Twas well, indeed, when warm with wine,
   To pledge them with a kindly tear,
   To talk them o'er, to wish them here,
To count their memories half divine;

But if they came who past away,
   Behold their brides in other hands;
   The hard heir strides about their lands,
And will not yield them for a day.

Yea, tho' their sons were none of these,
   Not less the yet-loved sire would make
   Confusion worse than death, and shake
The pillars of domestic peace.

Ah dear, but come thou back to me:
   Whatever change the years have wrought,
   I find not yet one lonely thought
That cries against my wish for thee.

XCI

When rosy plumelets tuft the larch,
   And rarely pipes the mounted thrush;
   Or underneath the barren bush
Flits by the sea-blue bird of March;

Come, wear the form by which I know
   Thy spirit in time among thy peers;
   The hope of unaccomplish'd years
Be large and lucid round thy brow.

When summer's hourly-mellowing change
   May breathe, with many roses sweet,
   Upon the thousand waves of wheat,
That ripple round the lonely grange;

Come: not in watches of the night,
   But where the sunbeam broodeth warm,
   Come, beauteous in thine after form,
And like a finer light in light.

XCII

If any vision should reveal
   Thy likeness, I might count it vain
   As but the canker of the brain;
Yea, tho' it spake and made appeal

To chances where our lots were cast
   Together in the days behind,
   I might but say, I hear a wind
Of memory murmuring the past.

Yea, tho' it spake and bared to view
   A fact within the coming year;
   And tho' the months, revolving near,
Should prove the phantom-warning true,

They might not seem thy prophecies,
   But spiritual presentiments,
   And such refraction of events
As often rises ere they rise.

XCIII

I shall not see thee. Dare I say
   No spirit ever brake the band
   That stays him from the native land
Where first he walk'd when claspt in clay?

No visual shade of some one lost,
   But he, the Spirit himself, may come
   Where all the nerve of sense is numb;
Spirit to Spirit, Ghost to Ghost.

O, therefore from thy sightless range
   With gods in unconjectured bliss,
   O, from the distance of the abyss
Of tenfold-complicated change,

Descend, and touch, and enter; hear
   The wish too strong for words to name;
   That in this blindness of the frame
My Ghost may feel that thine is near.

XCIV

How pure at heart and sound in head,
   With what divine affections bold
   Should be the man whose thought would hold
An hour's communion with the dead.

In vain shalt thou, or any, call
   The spirits from their golden day,
   Except, like them, thou too canst say,
My spirit is at peace with all.

They haunt the silence of the breast,
   Imaginations calm and fair,
   The memory like a cloudless air,
The conscience as a sea at rest:

But when the heart is full of din,
   And doubt beside the portal waits,
   They can but listen at the gates,
And hear the household jar within.

XCV

By night we linger'd on the lawn,
   For underfoot the herb was dry;
   And genial warmth; and o'er the sky
The silvery haze of summer drawn;

And calm that let the tapers burn
  Unwavering: not a cricket chirr'd:
  The brook alone far-off was heard,
And on the board the fluttering urn:

And bats went round in fragrant skies,
  And wheel'd or lit the filmy shapes
  That haunt the dusk, with ermine capes
And woolly breasts and beaded eyes;

While now we sang old songs that peal'd
  From knoll to knoll, where, couch'd at ease,
  The white kine glimmer'd, and the trees
Laid their dark arms about the field.

But when those others, one by one,
  Withdrew themselves from me and night,
  And in the house light after light
Went out, and I was all alone,

A hunger seized my heart; I read
  Of that glad year which once had been,
  In those fall'n leaves which kept their green,
The noble letters of the dead:

And strangely on the silence broke
  The silent-speaking words, and strange
  Was love's dumb cry defying change
To test his worth; and strangely spoke

The faith, the vigour, bold to dwell
  On doubts that drive the coward back,
  And keen thro' wordy snares to track
Suggestion to her inmost cell.

So word by word, and line by line,
  The dead man touch'd me from the past,
  And all at once it seem'd at last
The living soul was flash'd on mine,

And mine in this was wound, and whirl'd
  About empyreal heights of thought,
  And came on that which is, and caught
The deep pulsations of the world,

Æonian music measuring out
    The steps of time—the shocks of Chance—
    The blows of Death. At length my trance
Was cancell'd, stricken thro' with doubt.

Vague words! but ah, how hard to frame
    In matter-moulded forms of speech,
    Or ev'n for intellect to reach
Thro' memory that which I became:

Till now the doubtful dusk reveal'd
    The knolls once more where, couch'd at ease,
    The white kine glimmer'd, and the trees
Laid their dark arms about the field:

And suck'd from out the distant gloom
    A breeze began to tremble o'er
    The large leaves of the sycamore,
And fluctuate all the still perfume,

And gathering freshlier overhead,
    Rock'd the full-foliaged elms, and swung
    The heavy-folded rose, and flung
The lilies to and fro, and said,

"The dawn, the dawn," and diee away;
    And East and West, without a breath,
    Mixt their dim lights, like life and death,
To broaden into boundless day.

XCVI

You say, but with no touch of scorn,
    Sweet-hearted, you, whose light-blue eyes
    Are tender over drowning flies,
You tell me, doubt is Devil-born.

I know not: one indeed I knew
    In many a subtle question versed,
    Who touch'd a jarring lyre at first,
But ever strove to make it true:

Perplext in faith, but pure in deeds,
   At last he beat his music out.
   There lives more faith in honest doubt,
Believe me, than in half the creeds.

He fought his doubts and gather'd strength,
   He would not make his judgment blind,
   He faced the spectres of the mind
And laid them: thus he came at length

To find a stronger faith his own;
   And Power was with him in the night,
   Which makes the darkness and the light,
And dwells not in the light alone,

But in the darkness and the cloud,
   As over Sinaï's peaks of old,
   While Israel made their gods of gold,
Altho' the trumpet blew so loud.

XCVII

My love has talk'd with rocks and trees;
   He finds on misty mountain-ground
   His own vast shadow glory-crown'd;
He sees himself in all he sees.

Two partners of a married life—
   I look'd on these and thought of thee
   In vastness and in mystery,
And of my spirit as of a wife.

These two—they dwelt with eye on eye,
   Their hearts of old have beat in tune,
   Their meetings made December June
Their every parting was to die.

Their love has never past away;
   The days she never can forget
   Are earnest that he loves her yet,
Whate'er the faithless people say.

Her life is lone, he sits apart,
   He loves her yet, she will not weep,
   Tho' rapt in matters dark and deep
He seems to slight her simple heart.

He thrids the labyrinth of the mind,
   He reads the secret of the star,
   He seems so near and yet so far,
He looks so cold: she thinks him kind.

She keeps the gift of years before,
   A wither'd violet is her bliss:
   She knows not what his greatness is,
For that, for all, she loves him more.

For him she plays, to him she sings
   Of early faith and plighted vows;
   She knows but matters of the house,
And he, he knows a thousand things.

Her faith is fixt and cannot move,
   She darkly feels him great and wise,
   She dwells on him with faithful eyes,
"I cannot understand: I love."

XCVIII

You leave us: you will see the Rhine,
   And those fair hills I sail'd below,
   When I was there with him; and go
By summer belts of wheat and vine

To where he breathed his latest breath,
   That City. All her splendour seems
   No livelier than the wisp that gleams
On Lethe in the eyes of Death.

Let her great Danube rolling fair
   Enwind her isles, unmark'd of me:
   I have not seen, I will not see
Vienna; rather dream that there,

A treble darkness, Evil haunts
   The birth, the bridal; friend from friend
   Is oftener parted, fathers bend
Above more graves, a thousand wants

Gnarr at the heels of men, and prey
   By each cold hearth, and sadness flings
   Her shadow on the blaze of kings:
And yet myself have heard him say,

That not in any mother town
   With statelier progress to and fro
   The double tides of chariots flow
By park and suburb under brown

Of lustier leaves; nor more content,
   He told me, lives in any crowd,
   When all is gay with lamps, and loud
With sport and song, in booth and tent,

Imperial halls, or open plain;
   And wheels the circled dance, and breaks
   The rocket molten into flakes
Of crimson or in emerald rain.

XCIX

Risest thou thus, dim dawn, again,
   So loud with voices of the birds,
   So thick with lowings of the herds,
Day, when I lost the flower of men;

Who tremblest thro' thy darkling red
   On yon swoll'n brook that bubbles fast
   By meadows breathing of the past,
And woodlands holy to the dead;

Who murmurest in the foliaged eaves
   A song that slights the coming care,
   And Autumn laying here and there
A fiery finger on the leaves;

Who wakenest with thy balmy breath
   To myriads on the genial earth,
   Memories of bridal, or of birth,
And unto myriads more, of death.

O, wheresoever those may be,
   Betwixt the slumber of the poles,
   To-day they count as kindred souls;
They know me not, but mourn with me.

C

I climb the hill: from end to end
   Of all the landscape underneath,
   I find no place that does not breathe
Some gracious memory of my friend;

No gray old grange, or lonely fold,
   Or low morass and whispering reed,
   Or simple stile from mead to mead,
Or sheepwalk up the windy wold;

Nor hoary knoll of ash and hew
   That hears the latest linnet trill,
   Nor quarry trench'd along the hill
And haunted by the wrangling daw;

Nor runlet tinkling from the rock;
   Nor pastoral rivulet that swerves
   To left and right thro' meadowy curves,
That feed the mothers of the flock;

But each has pleased a kindred eye,
   And each reflects a kindlier day;
   And, leaving these, to pass away,
I think once more he seems to die.

CI

Unwatch'd, the garden bough shall sway,
   The tender blossom flutter down,
   Unloved, that beech will gather brown,
This maple burn itself away;

Unloved, the sun-flower, shining fair,
   Ray round with flames her disk of seed,
   And many a rose-carnation feed
With summer spice the humming air;

Unloved, by many a sandy bar,
   The brook shall babble down the plain,
   At noon or when the lesser wain
Is twisting round the polar star;

Uncared for, gird the windy grove,
   And flood the haunts of hern and crake;
   Or into silver arrows break
The sailing moon in creek and cove;

Till from the garden and the wild
   A fresh association blow,
   And year by year the landscape grow
Familiar to the stranger's child;

As year by year the labourer tills
   His wonted glebe, or lops the glades;
   And year by year our memory fades
From all the circle of the hills.

CII

We leave the well-beloved place
   Where first we gazed upon the sky;
   The roofs, that heard our earliest cry,
Will shelter one of stranger race.

We go, but ere we go from home,
   As down the garden-walks I move,
   Two spirits of a diverse love
Contend for loving masterdom.

One whispers, "Here thy boyhood sung
   Long since its matin song, and heard
   The low love-language of the bird
In native hazels tassel-hung."

The other answers, "Yea, but here
    Thy feet have stray'd in after hours
    With thy lost friend among the bowers,
And this hath made them trebly dear."

These two have striven half the day,
    And each prefers his separate claim,
    Poor rivals in a losing game,
That will not yield each other way.

I turn to go: my feet are set
    To leave the pleasant fields and farms;
    They mix in one another's arms
To one pure image of regret.

CIII

On that last night before we went
    From out the doors where I was bred,
    I dream'd a vision of the dead,
Which left my after-morn content.

Methought I dwelt within a hall,
    And maidens with me: distant hills
    From hidden summits fed with rills
A river sliding by the wall.

The hall with harp and carol rang.
    They sang of what is wise and good
    And graceful. In the centre stood
A statue veil'd, to which they sang;

And which, tho' veil'd, was known to me,
    The shape of him I loved, and love
    For ever: then flew in a dove
And brought a summons from the sea:

And when they learnt that I must go
    They wept and wail'd, but led the way
    To where a little shallop lay
At anchor in the flood below;

And on by many a level mead,
    And shadowing bluff that made the banks,
      We glided winding under ranks
Of iris, and the golden reed;

And still as vaster grew the shore
    And roll'd the floods in grander space,
      The maidens gather'd strength and grace
And presence, lordlier than before;

And I myself, who sat apart
    And watch'd them, wax'd in every limb;
      I felt the thews of Anakim,
The pulses of a Titan's heart;

As one would sing
    And one would chant the history
      Of that great race, which is to be,
And one the shaping of a star;

Until the forward-creeping tides
    Began to foam, and we to draw
      From deep to deep, to where we saw
A great ship lift her shining sides.

The man we loved was there on deck,
    But thrice as large as man he bent
      To greet us. Up the side I went,
And fell in silence on his neck;

Whereat those maidens with one mind
    Bewail'd their lot; I did them wrong:
      "We served thee here," they said, "so long,
And wilt thou leave us now behind?"

So rapt I was, they could not win
    An answer from my lips, but he
      Replying, "Enter likewise ye
And go with us:" they enter'd in.

And while the wind began to sweep
    A music out of sheet and shroud,
      We steer'd her toward a crimson cloud
That landlike slept along the deep.

CIV

The time draws near the birth of Christ;
   The moon is hid, the night is still;
   A single church below the hill
Is pealing, folded in the mist.

A single peal of bells below,
   That wakens at this hour of rest
   A single murmur in the breast,
That these are not the bells I know.

Like strangers' voices here they sound,
   In lands where not a memory strays,
   Nor landmark breathes of other days,
But all is new unhallow'd ground.

CV

To-night ungather'd let us leave
   This laurel, let this holly stand:
   We live within the stranger's land,
And strangely falls our Christmas-eve.

Our father's dust is left alone
   And silent under other snows:
   There in due time the woodbine blows,
The violet comes, but we are gone.

No more shall wayward grief abuse
   The genial hour with mask and mime;
   For change of place, like growth of time,
Has broke the bond of dying use.

Let cares that petty shadows cast,
   By which our lives are chiefly proved,
   A little spare the night I loved,
And hold it solemn to the past.

But let no footstep beat the floor,
   Nor bowl of wassail mantle warm;
   For who would keep an ancient form
Thro' which the spirit breathes no more?

Be neither song, nor game, nor feast;
   Nor harp be touch'd, nor flute be blown;
   No dance, no motion, save alone
What lightens in the lucid east

Of rising worlds by yonder wood.
   Long sleeps the summer in the seed;
   Run out your measured arcs, and lead
The closing cycle rich in good.

CVI

Ring out, wild bells, to the wild sky,
   The flying cloud, the frosty light:
   The year is dying in the night;
Ring out, wild bells, and let him die.

Ring out the old, ring in the new,
   Ring, happy bells, across the snow:
   The year is going, let him go;
Ring out the false, ring in the true.

Ring out the grief that saps the mind,
   For those that here we see no more;
   Ring out the feud of rich and poor,
Ring in redress to all mankind.

Ring out a slowly dying cause,
   And ancient forms of party strife;
   Ring in the nobler modes of life,
With sweeter manners, purer laws.

Ring out the want, the care, the sin,
   The faithless coldness of the times;
   Ring out, ring out my mournful rhymes,
But ring the fuller minstrel in.

Ring out false pride in place and blood,
   The civic slander and the spite;
   Ring in the love of truth and right,
Ring in the common love of good.

Ring out old shapes of foul disease;
    Ring out the narrowing lust of gold;
    Ring out the thousand wars of old,
Ring in the thousand years of peace.

Ring in the valiant man and free,
    The larger heart, the kindlier hand;
    Ring out the darkness of the land,
Ring in the Christ that is to be.

CVII

It is the day when he was born,
    A bitter day that early sank
    Behind a purple-frosty bank
Of vapour, leaving night forlorn.

The time admits not flowers or leaves
    To deck the banquet. Fiercely flies
    The blast of North and East, and ice
Makes daggers at the sharpen'd eaves,

And bristles all the brakes and thorns
    To yon hard crescent, as she hangs
    Above the wood which grides and clangs
Its leafless ribs and iron horns

Together, in the drifts that pass
    To darken on the rolling brine
    That breaks the coast. But fetch the wine,
Arrange the board and brim the glass;

Bring in great logs and let them lie,
    To make a solid core of heat;
    Be cheerful-minded, talk and treat
Of all things ev'n as he were by;

We keep the day. With festal cheer,
    With books and music, surely we
    Will drink to him, whate'er he be,
And sings he loved to hear.

CVIII

I will not shut me from my kind,
   And, lest I stiffen into stone,
   I will not eat my heart alone,
Nor feed with sighs a passing wind:

What profit lies in barren faith,
   And vacant yearning, tho' with might
   To scale the heaven's highest height,
Or dive below the wells of Death?

What find I in the highest place,
   But mine own phantom chanting hymns?
   And on the depths of death there swims
The reflex of a human face.

I'll rather take what fruit may be
   Of sorrow under human skies:
   'Tis held that sorrow makes us wise,
Whatever wisdom sleep with thee.

CIX

It is the day when he was born,
   A bitter day that early sank
   Behind a purple-frosty bank
Of vapour, leaving night forlorn.

The time admits not flowers or leaves
   To deck the banquet. Fiercely flies
   The blast of North and East, and ice
Makes daggers at the sharpen'd eaves,

And bristles all the brakes and thorns
   To yon hard crescent, as she hangs
   Above the wood which grides and clangs
Its leafless ribs and iron horns

Together, in the drifts that pass
   To darken on the rolling brine
   That breaks the coast. But fetch the wine,
Arrange the board and brim the glass;

Bring in great logs and let them lie,
  To make a solid core of heat;
  Be cheerful-minded, talk and treat
Of all things ev'n as he were by;

We keep the day. With festal cheer,
  With books and music, surely we
  Will drink to him, whate'er he be,
And sing the songs he loved to hear.

CX

Thy converse drew us with delight,
  The men of rathe and riper years:
  The feeble soul, a haunt of fears,
Forgot his weakness in thy sight.

On thee the loyal-hearted hung,
  The proud was half disarm'd of pride,
  Nor cared the serpent at thy side
To flicker with his double tongue.

The stern were mild when thou wert by,
  The flippant put himself to school
  And heard thee, and the brazen fool
Was soften'd, and he knew not why;

While I, thy nearest, sat apart,
  And felt thy triumph was as mine;
  And loved them more, that they were thine,
The graceful tact, the Christian art;

Nor mine the sweetness or the skill,
  But mine the love that will not tire,
  And, born of love, the vague desire
That spurs an imitative will.

CXI

The churl in spirit, up or down
  Along the scale of ranks, thro' all,
  To him who grasps a golden ball,
By blood a king, at heart a clown;

The churl in spirit, howe'er he veil
   His want in forms for fashion's sake,
   Will let his coltish nature break
At seasons thro' the gilded pale:

For who can always act? but he,
   To whom a thousand memories call,
   Not being less but more than all
The gentleness he seem'd to be,

Best seem'd the thing he was, and join'd
   Each office of the social hour
   To noble manners, as the flower
And native growth of noble mind;

Nor ever narrowness or spite,
   Or villain fancy fleeting by,
   Drew in the expression of an eye,
Where God and Nature met in light;

And thus he bore without abuse
   The grand old name of gentleman,
   Defamed by every charlatan,
And soil'd with all ignoble use.

CXII

High wisdom holds my wisdom less,
   That I, who gaze with temperate eyes
   On glorious insufficiencies,
Set light by narrower perfectness.

But thou, that fillest all the room
   Of all my love, art reason why
   I seem to cast a careless eye
On souls, the lesser lords of doom.

For what wert thou? some novel power
   Sprang up for ever at a touch,
   And hope could never hope too much,
In watching thee from hour to hour,

Large elements in order brought,
    And tracts of calm from tempest made,
    And world-wide fluctuation sway'd
In vassal tides that follow'd thought.

CXIII

'Tis held that sorrow makes us wise;
    Yet how much wisdom sleeps with thee
    Which not alone had guided me,
But served the seasons that may rise;

For can I doubt, who knew thee keen
    In intellect, with force and skill
    To strive, to fashion, to fulfil—
I doubt not what thou wouldst have been:

A life in civic action warm,
    A soul on highest mission sent,
    A potent voice of Parliament,
A pillar steadfast in the storm,

Should licensed boldness gather force,
    Becoming, when the time has birth,
    A lever to uplift the earth
And roll it in another course,

With thousand shocks that come and go,
    With agonies, with energies,
    With overthrowings, and with cries
And undulations to and fro.

CXIV

Who loves not Knowledge? Who shall rail
    Against her beauty? May she mix
    With men and prosper! Who shall fix
Her pillars? Let her work prevail.

But on her forehead sits a fire:
    She sets her forward countenance
    And leaps into the future chance,
Submitting all things to desire.

Half-grown as yet, a child, and vain—
   She cannot fight the fear of death.
   What is she, cut from love and faith,
But some wild Pallas from the brain

Of Demons? fiery-hot to burst
   All barriers in her onward race
   For power. Let her know her place;
She is the second, not the first.

A higher hand must make her mild,
   If all be not in vain; and guide
   Her footsteps, moving side by side
With wisdom, like the younger child:

For she is earthly of the mind,
   But Wisdom heavenly of the soul.
   O, friend, who camest to thy goal
So early, leaving me behind,

I would the great world grew like thee,
   Who grewest not alone in power
   And knowledge, but by year and hour
In reverence and in charity.

CXV

Now fades the last long streak of snow,
   Now burgeons every maze of quick
   About the flowering squares, and thick
By ashen roots the violets blow.

Now rings the woodland loud and long,
   The distance takes a lovelier hue,
   And drown'd in yonder living blue
The lark becomes a sightless song.

Now dance the lights on lawn and lea,
   The flocks are whiter down the vale,
   And milkier every milky sail
On winding stream or distant sea;

Where now the seamew pipes, or dives
  In yonder greening gleam, and fly
  The happy birds, that change their sky
To build and brood; that live their lives

From land to land; and in my breast
  Spring wakens too; and my regret
  Becomes an April violet,
And buds and blossoms like the rest.

CXVI

Is it, then, regret for buried time
  That keenlier in sweet April wakes,
  And meets the year, and gives and takes
The colours of the crescent prime?

Not all: the songs, the stirring air,
  The life re-orient out of dust
  Cry thro' the sense to hearten trust
In that which made the world so fair.

Not all regret: the face will shine
  Upon me, while I muse alone;
  And that dear voice, I once have known,
Still speak to me of me and mine:

Yet less of sorrow lives in me
  For days of happy commune dead;
  Less yearning for the friendship fled,
Than some strong bond which is to be.

CXVII

O days and hours, your work is this
  To hold me from my proper place,
  A little while from his embrace,
For fuller gain of after bliss:

That out of distance might ensue
  Desire of nearness doubly sweet;
  And unto meeting when we meet,
Delight a hundredfold accrue,

For every grain of sand that runs,
   And every span of shade that steals,
   And every kiss of toothed wheels,
And all the courses of the suns.

CXVIII

Contemplate all this work of Time,
   The giant labouring in his youth;
   Nor dream of human love and truth,
As dying Nature's earth and lime;

But trust that those we call the dead
   Are breathers of an ampler day
   For ever nobler ends. They say,
The solid earth whereon we tread

In tracts of fluent heat began,
   And grew to seeming-random forms,
   The seeming prey of cyclic storms,
Till at the last arose the man;

Who throve and branch'd from clime to clime,
   The herald of a higher race,
   And of himself in higher place,
If so he type this work of time

Within himself, from more to more;
   Or, crown'd with attributes of woe
   Like glories, move his course, and show
That life is not as idle ore,

But iron dug from central gloom,
   And heated hot with burning fears,
   And dipt in baths of hissing tears,
And batter'd with the shocks of doom

To shape and use. Arise and fly
   The reeling Faun, the sensual feast;
   Move upward, working out the beast,
And let the ape and tiger die.

CXIX

Doors, where my heart was used to beat
   So quickly, not as one that weeps
   I come once more; the city sleeps;
I smell the meadow in the street;

I hear a chirp of birds; I see
   Betwixt the black fronts long-withdrawn
   A light-blue lane of early dawn,
And think of early days and thee,

And bless thee, for thy lips are bland,
   And bright the friendship of thine eye;
   And in my thoughts with scarce a sigh
I take the pressure of thine hand.

CXX

I trust I have not wasted breath:
   I think we are not wholly brain,
   Magnetic mockeries; not in vain,
Like Paul with beasts, I fought with Death;

Not only cunning casts in clay:
   Let Science prove we are, and then
   What matters Science unto men,
At least to me? I would not stay.

Let him, the wiser man who springs
   Hereafter, up from childhood shape
   His action like the greater ape,
But I was *born* to other things.

CXXI

Sad Hesper o'er the buried sun
   And ready, thou, to die with him,
   Thou watchest all things ever dim
And dimmer, and a glory done:

The team is loosen'd from the wain,
    The boat is drawn upon the shore;
    Thou listenest to the closing door,
And life is darken'd in the brain.

Bright Phosphor, fresher for the night,
    By thee the world's great work is heard
    Beginning, and the wakeful bird;
Behind thee comes the greater light:

The market boat is on the stream,
    And voices hail it from the brink;
    Thou hear'st the village hammer clink,
And see'st the moving of the team.

Sweet Hesper-Phosphor, double name
    For what is one, the first, the last,
    Thou, like my present and my past,
Thy place is changed; thou art the same.

CXXII

Oh, wast thou with me, dearest, then,
    While I rose up against my doom,
    And yearn'd to burst the folded gloom,
To bare the eternal Heavens again,

To feel once more, in placid awe,
    The strong imagination roll
    A sphere of stars about my soul,
In all her motion one with law;

If thou wert with me, and the grave
    Divide us not, be with me now,
    And enter in at breast and brow,
Till all my blood, a fuller wave,

Be quicken'd with a livelier breath,
    And like an inconsiderate boy,
    As in the former flash of joy,
I slip the thoughts of life and death;

And all the breeze of Fancy blows,
   And every dew-drop paints a bow,
   The wizard lightnings deeply glow,
And every thought breaks out a rose.

CXXIII

There rolls the deep where grew the tree.
   O earth, what changes hast thou seen!
   There where the long street roars, hath been
The stillness of the central sea.

The hills are shadows, and they flow
   From form to form, and nothing stands;
   They melt like mist, the solid lands,
Like clouds they shape themselves and go.

But in my spirit will I dwell,
   And dream my dream, and hold it true;
   For tho' my lips may breathe adieu,
I cannot think the thing farewell.

CXXIV

That which we dare invoke to bless;
   Our dearest faith; our ghastliest doubt;
   He, They, One, All; within, without;
The Power in darkness whom we guess;

I found Him not in world or sun,
   Or eagle's wing, or insect's eye;
   Nor thro' the questions men may try,
The petty cobwebs we have spun:

If e'er when faith had fall'n asleep,
   I heard a voice "believe no more"
   And heard an ever-breaking shore
That tumbled in the Godless deep;

A warmth within the breast would melt
   The freezing reason's colder part,
   And like a man in wrath the heart
Stood up and answer'd "I have felt."

No, like a child in doubt and fear:
   But that blind clamour made me wise;
   Then was I as a child that cries,
But, crying, knows his father near;

And what I am beheld again
   What is, and no man understands;
   And out of darkness came the hands
That reach thro' nature, moulding men.

CXXV

Whatever I have said or sung,
   Some bitter notes my harp would give,
   Yea, tho' there often seem'd to live
A contradiction on the tongue,

Yet Hope had never lost her youth;
   She did but look through dimmer eyes;
   Or Love but play'd with gracious lies,
Because he felt so fix'd in truth:

And if the song were full of care,
   He breathed the spirit of the song;
   And if the words were sweet and strong
He set his royal signet there;

Abiding with me till I sail
   To seek thee on the mystic deeps,
   And this electric force, that keeps
A thousand pulses dancing, fail.

CXXVI

Love is and was my Lord and King,
   And in his presence I attend
   To hear the tidings of my friend,
Which every hour his couriers bring.

Love is and was my King and Lord,
   And will be, tho' as yet I keep
   Within his court on earth, and sleep
Encompass'd by his faithful guard,

And hear at times a sentinel
   Who moves about from place to place,
   And whispers to the worlds of space,
In the deep night, that all is well.

CXXVII

And all is well, tho' faith and form
   Be sunder'd in the night of fear;
   Well roars the storm to those that hear
A deeper voice across the storm,

Proclaiming social truth shall spread,
   And justice, ev'n tho' thrice again
   The red fool-fury of the Seine
Should pile her barricades with dead.

But ill for him that wears a crown,
   And him, the lazar, in his rags:
   They tremble, the sustaining crags;
The spires of ice are toppled down,

And molten up, and roar in flood;
   The fortress crashes from on high,
   The brute earth lightens to the sky,
And the great Aeon sinks in blood,

And compass'd by the fires of Hell;
   While thou, dear spirit, happy star,
   O'erlook'st the tumult from afar,
And smilest, knowing all is well.

CXXVIII

The love that rose on stronger wings,
   Unpalsied when he met with Death,
   Is comrade of the lesser faith
That sees the course of human things.

No doubt vast eddies in the flood
   Of onward time shall yet be made,
   And throned races may degrade;
Yet, O ye mysteries of good,

Wild Hours that fly with Hope and Fear,
  If all your office had to do
  With old results that look like new;
If this were all your mission here,

To draw, to sheathe a useless sword,
  To fool the crowd with glorious lies,
  To cleave a creed in sects and cries,
To change the bearing of a word,

To shift an arbitrary power,
  To cramp the student at his desk,
  To make old bareness picturesque
And tuft with grass a feudal tower;

Why then my scorn might well descend
  On you and yours. I see in part
  That all, as in some piece of art,
Is toil cöoperant to an end.

CXXIX

Dear friend, far off, my lost desire,
  So far, so near in woe and weal;
  O loved the most, when most I feel
There is a lower and a higher;

Known and unknown; human, divine;
  Sweet human hand and lips and eye;
  Dear heavenly friend that canst not die,
Mine, mine, for ever, ever mine;

Strange friend, past, present, and to be;
  Loved deeplier, darklier understood;
  Behold, I dream a dream of good,
And mingle all the world with thee.

CXXX

Thy voice is on the rolling air;
  I hear thee where the waters run;
  Thou standest in the rising sun,
And in the setting thou art fair.

What art thou then? I cannot guess;
   But tho' I seem in star and flower
   To feel thee some diffusive power,
I do not therefore love thee less:

My love involves the love before;
   My love is vaster passion now;
   Tho' mix'd with God and Nature thou,
I seem to love thee more and more.

Far off thou art, but ever nigh;
   I have thee still, and I rejoice;
   I prosper, circled with thy voice;
I shall not lose thee tho' I die.

CXXXI

O living will that shalt endure
   When all that seems shall suffer shock,
   Rise in the spiritual rock,
Flow thro' our deeds and make them pure,

That we may lift from out of dust
   A voice as unto him that hears,
   A cry above the conquer'd years
To one that with us works, and trust,

With faith that comes of self-control,
   The truths that never can be proved
   Until we close with all we loved,
And all we flow from, soul in soul.

EPILOGUE

O true and tried, so well and long,
   Demand not thou a marriage lay;
   In that it is thy marriage day
Is music more than any song.

Nor have I felt so much of bliss
   Since first he told me that he loved
   A daughter of our house; nor proved
Since that dark day a day like this;

Tho' I since then have number'd o'er
   Some thrice three years: they went and came,
   Remade the blood and changed the frame,
And yet is love not less, but more;

No longer caring to embalm
   In dying is a dead regret,
   But like a statue solid-set,
And moulded in colossal calm.

Regret is dead, but love is more
   Than in the summers that are flown,
   For I myself with these have grown
To something greater than before;

Which makes appear the songs I made
   As echoes out of weaker times,
   As half but idle brawling rhymes,
The sport of random sun and shade.

But where is she, the bridal flower,
   That must be made a wife ere noon?
   She enters, glowing like the moon
Of Eden on its bridal bower:

On me she bends her blissful eyes
   And then on thee; they meet thy look
   And brighten like the star that shook
Betwixt the palms of paradise.

O when her life was yet in bud,
   He too foretold the perfect rose.
   For thee she grew, for thee she grows
For ever, and as fair as good.

And thou art worthy; full of power;
   As gentle; liberal-minded, great,
   Consistent; wearing all that weight
Of learning lightly like a flower.

But now set out: the noon is near,
   And I must give away the bride;
   She fears not, or with thee beside
And me behind her, will not fear.

For I that danced her on my knee,
    That watch'd her on her nurse's arm,
    That shielded all her life from harm
At last must part with her to thee;

Now waiting to be made a wife,
    Her feet, my darling, on the dead
    Their pensive tablets round her head,
And the most living words of life

Breathed in her ear. The ring is on,
    The "wilt thou" answer'd, and again
    The "wilt thou" ask'd, till out of twain
Her sweet "I will" has made you one.

Now sign your names, which shall be read,
    Mute symbols of a joyful morn,
    By village eyes as yet unborn;
The names are sign'd, and overhead

Begins the clash and clang that tells
    The joy to every wandering breeze;
    The blind wall rocks, and on the trees
The dead leaf trembles to the bells.

O happy hour, and happier hours
    Await them. Many a merry face
    Salutes them—maidens of the place,
That pelt us in the porch with flowers.

O happy hour, behold the bride
    With him to whom her hand I gave.
    They leave the porch, they pass the grave
That has to-day its sunny side.

To-day the grave is bright for me,
    For them the light of life increased,
    Who stay to share the morning feast,
Who rest to-night beside the sea.

Let all my genial spirits advance
    To meet and greet a whiter sun;
    My drooping memory will not shun
The foaming grape of eastern France.

It circles round, and fancy plays,
   And hearts are warm'd and faces bloom,
   As drinking health to bride and groom
We wish them store of happy days.

Nor count me all to blame if I
   Conjecture of a stiller guest,
   Perchance, perchance, among the rest,
And, tho' in silence, wishing joy.

But they must go, the time draws on,
   And those white-favour'd horses wait;
   They rise, but linger; it is late;
Farewell, we kiss, and they are gone.

A shade falls on us like the dark
   From little cloudlets on the grass,
   But sweeps away as out we pass
To range the woods, to roam the park,

Discussing how their courtship grew,
   And talk of others that are wed,
   And how she look'd, and what he said,
And back we come at fall of dew.

Again the feast, the speech, the glee,
   The shade of passing thought, the wealth
   Of words and wit, the double health,
The crowning cup, the three-times-three,

And last the dance;—till I retire:
   Dumb is that tower which spake so loud,
   And high in heaven the streaming cloud,
And on the downs a rising fire:

And rise, O moon, from yonder down,
   Till over down and over dale
   All night the shining vapour sail
And pass the silent-lighted town,

The white-faced halls, the glancing rills,
   And catch at every mountain head,
   And o'er the friths that branch and spread
Their sleeping silver thro' the hills;

And touch with shade the bridal doors,
   With tender gloom the roof, the wall;
   And breaking let the splendour fall
To spangle all the happy shores

By which they rest, and ocean sounds,
   And, star and system rolling past,
   A soul shall draw from out the vast
And strike his being into bounds,

And, moved thro' life of lower phase,
   Result in man, be born and think,
   And act and love, a closer link
Betwixt us and the crowning race

Of those that, eye to eye, shall look
   On knowledge; under whose command
   Is Earth and Earth's, and in their hand
Is Nature like an open book;

No longer half-akin to brute,
   For all we thought and loved and did,
   And hoped, and suffer'd, is but seed
Of what in them is flower and fruit;

Whereof the man, that with me trod
   This planet, was a noble type
   Appearing ere the times were ripe,
That friend of mine who lives in God,

That God, which ever lives and loves,
   One God, one law, one element,
   And one far-off divine event,
To which the whole creation moves.

THE END

www.ingramcontent.com/pod-product-compliance
Lightning Source LLC
Chambersburg PA
CBHW031413040426
42444CB00005B/547